Y0-CBA-441

Some never consider that all humanity is not only destined to die, but that our future includes standing before the God of this universe to give an account. Rabbi Greg Hershberg's book, *Don't Die in Your Sins*, tackles both death and what lies beyond it. We need a Savior who will be waiting on the other side of the grave, one who can guide us safely home. That Savior's name is Jesus (Yeshua in Hebrew). He is the answer for life today and life in eternity. But how do we come to know this Savior and assure ourselves of a positive outcome? The answer is within these pages.

Dr. H. Dean Haun
Senior Pastor, First Baptist Church, Morristown, Tennessee
President and Founder, Harvest of Israel
Former President of the Tennessee Baptist Convention

Rabbi Greg Hershberg has written a practical and easy-to-read book that will help you better understand the gospel and will strengthen your faith.

Rabbi Jonathan Bernis
President and CEO, Jewish Voice Ministries

DON'T DIE IN YOUR SINS

DON'T DIE IN YOUR SINS

A Simple Explanation of the
Best News Known to Mankind

GREG HERSHBERG

ANEKO
PRESS

www.getzel.org

Don't Die in Your Sins

© 2023 by Greg Hershberg

All rights reserved. Published 2023.

Cover Designer: J. Martin

Editor: Paul Miller

Aneko Press

www.anekopress.com

Aneko Press, Life Sentence Publishing, and our logos are trademarks of Life Sentence Publishing, Inc.
203 E. Birch Street
P.O. Box 652
Abbotsford, WI 54405

RELIGION / Christian Theology / Soteriology

Paperback ISBN: 979-8-88936-226-5

eBook ISBN: 979-8-88936-227-2

10   9   8   7

Available where books are sold

CONTENTS

MY INTRODUCTION TO DEATH

I remember it like it was yesterday. I was sitting in a bathtub as an eight-year-old boy and overhearing my mom crying as she told my dad that my grandmother had died. It made me so sad not only to hear my mother crying, but also to know that I would never see my grandmother again. Even though I knew very little about death and dying, I knew enough to know that she was gone forever. She was my last living grandparent, and it hurt so much. Not only was she my last living grandparent, but she was a beautiful person with a gentle spirit, and she always made me feel loved.

No one ever spoke to me about death, and I never had anyone close to me die, so I really did not know much about what happens to a person after death. Death is a subject that most of us don't like to think about or talk about, yet sadly enough, we all experience it. In fact, most of us lose many friends, family members, and other loved ones throughout our lives. It is a sad reality that we don't like to face. Even when a person dies, we tend to use terminology that will soften the blow. We say things such as, "She passed," "He is in a better place," or "He went home." The fact of the matter is that the person died.

There are many reasons why so many people are afraid to die. One reason is the fear of the unknown. Death remains the ultimate unknown because no one in human history has survived it to tell us what really happens after we take our last breath. There are some people out there who claim to have died and then went either to heaven or hell, but since there is no scientific proof to back up their stories, they are not widely accepted. It is human nature to want to understand and make sense of the world around us.

Many people fear the idea that they will completely cease to exist.

Another reason why people are afraid of death is the fear of non-existence. Many people fear the idea that they will completely cease to exist. We might typically associate this fear with atheists or others who do not have personal spiritual or religious beliefs. However, many people of faith also worry that their belief in an afterlife may not be true after all or that they did not earn eternal life while alive. Yes, even people of faith struggle with the idea of death and the afterlife.

Then there is the fear of eternal punishment. Similar to the fear of non-existence, this belief does not apply just to devout religious people or sincere spiritual believers. Many people, regardless of their religious persuasion or lack of spiritual beliefs, fear that they will be punished for what they did or did not do while here on earth. They have this innate sense that they will have to pay for their wrongdoings.

There is also the fear of the loss of control. Human nature generally seeks to control the situations we encounter, but death remains something over which basically we have no control. This frightens many people. Some people may attempt to exert some form of control over death by behaving in an extremely careful manner to avoid risks or by undergoing rigorous, frequent health checks, but the fact of the matter is that every single person still dies.

Lastly, there is the fear of what will become of our loved ones. Another very common fear surrounding death focuses on the concern of what will happen to those entrusted to our care if we die. Parents, for example, might worry about a newborn or other child. Family members who provide home care to a loved one might fear that no one else can handle their patient's many needs and demands. Someone in the prime of life might feel afraid at the thought of leaving a spouse alone due to death.

A healthy fear of death can remind us to make the most of our time here on earth and not to take our relationships here for granted. Fearing the reality of death might also push us to work harder in order to leave a lasting legacy. George Bernard Shaw summed it up well by saying, "I want to be thoroughly used up when I die, for the harder I work, the more I live."[1] With that being said, death is somewhat of an enigma that desperately needs to be discussed no matter the cost, considering we will all die.

---

1   George Bernard Shaw, *Man and Superman*, Act IV (London: Royal Court Theatre, 1905).

DEATH IS UNAVOIDABLE

It is a good thing to talk to your children about death. When they are old enough for you to talk to them about sexuality, they are old enough for you to talk to them about death – and it is very important for you to do so.

I was always athletic and a fitness enthusiast. There was hardly a sport I did not play. I loved the competition, as well as the feeling I got from the exercise itself. Little did I know that when you exercise, your brain releases endorphins. Endorphins are chemicals (hormones) your body releases when it feels pain or stress. They are released during pleasurable activities such as exercise, eating, and sexual activity. Endorphins help relieve pain, reduce stress, and improve one's sense of well-being. Endorphins are basically natural pain relievers. They are "feel good" chemicals because they can make you feel better and put you in a positive state of mind. To this day, I need to exercise – not so much for the physical benefit, but rather for the feel-good reward.

My wife was also an athlete in school, as well as later becoming an aerobics instructor and personal trainer. In fact, we met at a fitness center in New York. I was at a stage in my life where I wanted to remain single. I had just finished a serious relationship that didn't work out for a multitude of reasons, so I just needed a break. But one look at this ravishing beauty behind the reception desk of the Jack LaLanne Fitness Center, and I was in la-la land.

Once we got married and began a family, it was only natural that our children would be introduced to fitness as part of their lifestyle. I got my sons involved in sports, as well as in lifting weights. They really took to it, and they became regulars at the gym. They soon became well aware of their strength, so they lifted hard and heavy and began to develop their bodies – so much so that the last time I wrestled with them, my rotator cuff tore – and I'm no lightweight. Despite the fact that my shoulder will never be the same, I was pretty proud of their efforts. At the same time, I felt as though they needed to know that one day their strength will be gone and their bodies will lie in a grave. As maudlin and depressing as that may sound, it is a discussion that needs to be had.

My daughters were also very athletic. They also trained in sports and became competitive athletes. I do not want to sound sexist, but they were also becoming aware of their looks, so they began to put on makeup. They needed to know that one day these looks will be gone and their bodies will also lie in a grave. Help your children see that caring for their bodies is important, but caring for their souls matters even more. I hear many parents talk about their children being smart and being great athletes, but I don't hear enough parents talking about how wonderful their children's character is or how compassionate they are or how Christlike they are. Like the Bible says, *Although physical exercise does have some value, godliness is valuable for everything, since it holds promise both for the present life and for the life to come* (1 Timothy 4:8).

It is my opinion that every person should attend at least one funeral a year. We all love going to weddings: the joy, the jubilation, the celebration – they are so much fun. Weddings are all about life – and death and dying are nowhere to be found. On the other hand, going to a funeral reminds us that life is but a vapor (James 4:14), and one day our own lives will be gone as well. At a funeral, death smacks you right in the face; you just can't escape it. When I hear an

> Going to a funeral reminds us that life is but a vapor, and one day our own lives will be gone as well.

announcement that someone has died, I try to remember that one day that someone will be me.

I got a real taste of the brevity of life early on. Both of my grandfathers had died before I was born, so I never got to meet them. My two grandmothers died before I was ten years old.

Death hit me really hard at the age of fifteen when my dad died. My dad had a very tough life. He lost his father when he was very young. Just a few years later, at the age of ten, the Great Depression of 1929 hit. He never got to enjoy what I would call a normal childhood. At the age of twenty-one, he joined the Rangers to fight in World War II. He was awarded the Bronze Star for bravery, and also received a Purple Heart. He was also reported as missing in action, so you can only imagine the PTSD that he came home with. There were no counseling sessions back then. They just came home and got jobs so they could make ends meet.

My father worked on the loading dock and never got out of the projects. His work was laborious and mindless. For him, it was all about taking care of his family. He was a strong man, and I always felt as if nothing bad could ever happen to me as long as he was around. In other words, I felt completely safe and secure with him around. He had an opportunity to retire early, so he jumped on it. All he wanted to do was go to a few baseball games, listen to some jazz music, and read the newspaper from front to back.

After he retired, I remember him saying, "Greg, I beat the system." Little did he know that he would die a few weeks later. I will never forget the sight of two strange men coming into our little apartment and then carrying my dad past me in a long black bag.

Again, I didn't know much about death – except the fact that my dad was gone and I would never see him again. The message that was drilled into my head that day was that life is short, so I should live it up; and live it up, I did. I lived life in the fast lane. I never banked on tomorrow, so I really did live life just for the day. I was not concerned about tomorrow. My dad had a saying: "Live life every day like it's your last day because one day it's gonna be." However, I always had the fear of death looming over me. All I knew was that you have only one life, so you better live it up!

People die in many ways. Some die in war or through acts of violence. Some die through illnesses, heart attacks, or cancer. Still others die from old age. The timing of death is different. Some people die early in life while others live a long time. These things are important, but they are not the ultimate things. I came to realize that the most important thing to think about is what happens to us after death.

For most people, death is either the great mystery or the great denial. People either avoid the subject entirely or they just say, "No one knows, so just live your life." Those who do not believe in God may take the position that this life is the only one that we have and the only one that counts, so they believe that they should just live it up. Most of us sleep a third of our lives away, and we work another third. This means that two-thirds of our lives are used up sleeping and working, so we really only have a third of our lives to ourselves. If we break down that third, we have responsibilities, sicknesses, and chores that chip away at the time. According to World Population Review,[2] in 2023 there were 332,648 deaths per day in the world. That is 13,860 per hour, or 231 deaths every minute.

> Those who do not believe in God may take the position that this life is the only one we have, so they should just live it up.

However, what if this is not all there is? What if there is a God, and what if the Bible really is true? That would mean that there is, in fact, life after death.

---

2   2023 World Population Review, *https://worldpopulationreview.com*.

IS THERE LIFE AFTER DEATH?

People plan more for the future now than ever before. They plan with pensions, 401Ks, IRAs, Social Security, life insurance, and the list goes on. But where does our future end? Fifty-two percent of Americans believe in heaven and hell, while only thirty-seven percent of Americans believe in a bodily resurrection of the dead. The book of Job asks a simple question about the afterlife: *If a man dies, will he live again?* (Job 14:14). Asking the question is easy, but it's not so easy finding someone to answer the question with authority and experience.

Jesus is the one person who can speak with any real authority and experience regarding the afterlife. What gives Him sole authority to speak about heaven is that He came from there. Jesus was not merely a human teacher sent from God. Jesus was one who lived with God from all eternity and came down into the world. No human being had access to the presence of God continually in the way that He had. He could ascend to God's dwelling place in a very unique way because He had descended out of heaven to earth in the first place.

Jesus, with His firsthand experience in heaven, presents us with three basic truths about the subject of life after death:

1. There is life after death.

2. There are two destinations from which everyone must choose.

3. There is a way to ensure you make the right choice.

In the twelfth chapter of Mark, when Jesus had an encounter with the Sadducees, He affirmed that there is an afterlife. The Sadducees were the freethinkers of their day, like liberals are today. They were wealthy and held positions of power, including that of the chief priest. They built a system of doubt and denial through tolerance (where anything goes) and relativism (where truth is whatever you want it to be). They came to Jesus with a preposterous story, trying to ridicule the whole idea of bodily resurrection. They reminded Jesus that the Law of God made a special provision for the widows in Israel. In order to preserve the family line, the Law stipulated that if a man died childless, his brother should marry the widow. *If brothers live together, and one of them dies childless, his widow is not to marry someone unrelated to him; her husband's brother is to go to her and perform the duty of a brother-in-law by marrying her* (Deuteronomy 25:5).

They said to Jesus, "Suppose a woman married a man, and he died. The man had six brothers, and the woman married the next brother, who also died. All six of her first husband's brothers died after she married them. Finally, she died." Now for the clever question. They asked, "In the resurrection, whose wife will she be?" They thought they were smart, but the Savior told them that they were abysmally ignorant of both the Scriptures, which teach resurrection, and the power of God, which raises the dead.

Picture the scene. Here were the social elite, the intelligentsia, the power mongers. They were the aristocrats, politically connected with Rome, as well as with the temple in Jerusalem. They did not relate well to the commoner, nor did the commoner relate well to them. Jesus, a commoner from the lowly esteemed town of poor Nazareth, comes along and has the audacity to tell them that they were lost.

First of all, they should have known that the marriage relationship does not continue in heaven (Matthew 22:30). Then Jesus took the Sadducees, who valued the law of Moses above the rest of the Old Testament, back to the account of Moses at the burning bush (Exodus 3:6), where God spoke of Himself as the God of Abraham, Isaac, and Jacob. Jesus used this to show that God was the God of the living, not the God of the dead. But how so? Weren't Abraham, Isaac, and Jacob long gone – dead – by the time God appeared to Moses?

Yes, their bodies were buried in the cave of Machpelah in Hebron. How, then, is God the God of the living? The argument seems to be that God had made promises to the patriarchs (Abraham, Isaac, and Jacob) concerning the Messiah. These promises were not fulfilled in their lifetimes. When God spoke to Moses at the burning bush, the bodies of the patriarchs were in the grave, yet God spoke of Himself as the God of the living. Since God cannot lie, He must fulfill His promises to Abraham, Isaac, and Jacob.

Resurrection is an absolute necessity from what we know of the character of God.

Therefore, resurrection is an absolute necessity from what we know of the character of God.

In the fourteenth chapter of the book of John, Jesus comforted His disciples by telling them, and us, about the afterlife: *Don't let yourselves be disturbed. Trust in God and trust in me. In my Father's house are many places to live. If there weren't, I would have told you; because I am going there to prepare a place for you. Since I am going and preparing a place for you, I will return to take you with me; so that where I am, you may be also* (John 14:1-3). Jesus told them that He was going away and that they would not be able to see Him. He said, "You believe in God, and yet you do not see Him, so believe in Me in the same way." The Father's home refers to heaven, where there are many dwelling places. There is room there for all the redeemed. If it were not so, the Lord would have told them. He would not have them build on false hopes.

Jesus said, *I am going there to prepare a place for you.* The Lord went back to heaven to prepare a place. We do not know very much about this place, but we do know that provision is being made for every child of God. The bottom line is that it is described as a wonderful place where there is no pain, no sorrow, no suffering, and no death (Revelation 21:4). About this place, we can finally say, "It's all good," and mean it. *Since I am going and preparing a place for you, I will return to take you with me; so that where I am, you may be also.* This refers to the time when the Lord will come back again. Those who have died in faith will be raised when the living will be changed and when all the believers in Jesus will be taken to heaven. This is a personal, literal coming of the Messiah. As surely as He went away, He will come again.

You cannot discuss life, death, and the afterlife without mentioning the parable of the rich man and Lazarus (Luke 16:19-31). This is the quintessential story when discussing the afterlife. In this story, we have some of the greatest contrasts, if not *the* greatest contrast, the Bible has to offer. We have two lives, two deaths, and two afterlives. Let's have a look:

Jesus said, "There was a certain rich man who was

splendidly clothed in purple and fine linen and who lived each day in luxury. At his gate lay a poor man named Lazarus who was covered with sores. As Lazarus lay there longing for scraps from the rich man's table, the dogs would come and lick his open sores.

"Finally, the poor man died and was carried by the angels to sit beside Abraham at the heavenly banquet. The rich man also died and was buried, and he went to the place of the dead. There, in torment, he saw Abraham in the far distance with Lazarus at his side.

"The rich man shouted, 'Father Abraham, have some pity! Send Lazarus over here to dip the tip of his finger in water and cool my tongue. I am in anguish in these flames.'

"But Abraham said to him, 'Son, remember that during your lifetime you had everything you wanted, and Lazarus had nothing. So now he is here being comforted, and you are in anguish. And besides, there is a great chasm separating us. No one can cross over to you from here, and no one can cross over to us from there.'

"Then the rich man said, 'Please, Father Abraham, at least send him to my father's home. For I have five brothers, and I want him to warn them so they don't end up in this place of torment.'

"But Abraham said, 'Moses and the prophets have warned them. Your brothers can read what they wrote.'

"The rich man replied, 'No, Father Abraham! But if someone is sent to them from the dead, then they will repent of their sins and turn to God.'

"But Abraham said, 'If they won't listen to Moses and the prophets, they won't be persuaded even if someone rises from the dead.'" (Luke 16:19-31 NLT)

First we have the rich man. He wears the finest clothes – robes of purple made from Tyrian dye and expensive linen shirts made from Egyptian cotton. His home is an estate with lush, manicured gardens. Inside the palatial estate is the finest furniture, along with priceless works of art. The Italian marble floors are magnificent, reflecting one's image with a high sheen that his guests certainly loved. His table is a smorgasbord of gourmet foods – the finest meats, fowl, and seafood money can buy, the choicest fruits and vegetables, and the finest wines from the world's best vineyards. This is how the rich man lives day in and day out.

Then there is Lazarus, the beggar. Dumped at the rich man's gate like a sack of garbage, he was probably brought there by those who wanted him out of their neighborhood. He is pitiful, like a bag of bones, emaciated with hunger. His body is covered in oozing sores, and he is plagued by the unclean dogs that come to lick his wounds.

Who will stop and help such misery? Who will feed him, bathe him, and clothe him? Who will take him in and give him shelter for the night? Who will clean his sores? Who will hold his hand and listen to the story of his life? Who?

The rich man lives for himself, catering to his bodily pleasures and appetites. He has no genuine love for God and no care for his fellow man. Lazarus hopes that maybe, just maybe, one of the guests at the many parties the rich man throws might bring him some table scraps as they are leaving. But sadly enough, at the rich man's estate, mercy is in short supply. None of the guests want to look at him, let alone come near him or touch him. Lazarus watches them come and go, and they ignore him.

All of a sudden, what he thinks is the tongues of dogs licking his sores becomes the hands of angels. The beggar died and was carried off by angels to Abraham's side. Many people question whether angels actually participate in carrying the souls of believers to heaven, but there is no reason to doubt the plain force of the words. Angels minister to believers in this life, and there is no reason why they would not do so at the time of death. "Abraham's side" is a symbolic expression to denote the place of bliss. To any Jewish person, the thought of enjoying fellowship with Abraham would suggest inexpressible joy. "Abraham's bosom" is just another name for heaven.

> **Angels minister to believers in this life, and there is no reason why they would not do so at the time of death.**

So not only was the rich man's body buried in death, but his soul, or conscious self, went to Hades, which is the abode of the unsaved. Since the rich man was in torment, we need to make a couple of points:

1. It should be made clear that the unnamed rich man was not necessarily condemned to Hades because of his wealth. By his careless disregard of the beggar who was laid at his gate, this particular rich man showed that he did not have true saving faith. If he had the love of God in him, he could not have lived in luxury, comfort, and ease while a fellow man was outside his front door begging for a few crumbs of bread. It must have come as a shock to the disciples that the rich man went to Hades, as they were taught that riches were a sign of God's blessing and favor.

2. It is likewise true that it was not Lazarus's poverty that caused him to be saved. Lazarus was saved because he had trusted the Lord for the salvation of his soul. Poverty is not necessarily a virtue. This narrative proves that there is conscious existence beyond the grave. In fact, we are struck by the extent of knowledge that the rich man had. He saw Abraham in the distance and Lazarus at his side. He was even able to communicate with Abraham. Calling him *Father Abraham*, he begged for mercy, pleading that Lazarus might bring him a drop of water to cool his tongue.

The patriarch reminded the rich man of his lifetime of luxury, ease, and indulgence. He also recounted the poverty and suffering of Lazarus. Now, beyond the grave, the tables were turned. The inequalities of earth were reversed. Lazarus, once dumped in torment outside the gates of the rich man's estate, now saw the rich man dumped outside of heaven's gate, lying in torment of his own. We learn here that the choices of this life determine our eternal destiny. Once death has occurred, that destiny is fixed. There is no passage from the abode of the saved to that of the damned, or vice versa. In the midst of all the technicalities, let us not miss the message of the story: it is better to beg for bread on earth than to beg for water in Hades.

DEATH

eath is the most misunderstood part of life. It is not a great sleep, but a great awakening. It is the moment when we awaken, rub our eyes, and see things as God has seen them all along.

Death can be thought of as separation. Physical death is the separation of the body from the soul, while spiritual death is the separation of the soul from God. Jesus taught that we should not fear physical death, but we should be most concerned about spiritual death (Matthew 10:28). For non-believers who have died, Hades is a disembodied state of conscious punishment, a state of suffering. It is a sort of holding tank, an intermediate condition where they await the final judgment of God. Hell is the final prison of the wicked dead. The deciding factor at this judgment is whether one has died in his or her sins or whether one has died in the Lord.

G. B. Hardy, a world-renowned mathematician and brilliant scientist specializing in population genetics, once said, "I have only two questions to ask. One, has anyone ever defeated death? Two, did he make a way for me to do it also?"[3] The answer to both of Hardy's questions is a resounding yes. One person has both defeated death and provided a way for everyone who puts their trust in Him to overcome death as well. No one who trusts in Jesus Christ needs to fear death. The Word of God instructs us that through faith in Jesus, we have victory over death and the grave. In other words, the believer in Jesus Christ can say with humble confidence, "Hey death – who is afraid of you now?" But can we really trust the Word of God?

No one who trusts in Jesus Christ needs to fear death.

---

3   G. B. Hardy, *Countdown: A Time to Choose* (Chicago: Moody Press, 1972).

CAN I TRUST THE BIBLE?

"**M**any people refuse to believe without some evidence, as indeed they should. Since God created us as rational beings He does not expect us to live irrationally. He wants us to look before we leap," Norman Leo Geisler, a Christian systematic theologian and Christian apologist, said. "This does not mean there is no room for faith. But God wants us to take a step of faith in the light of evidence, rather than to leap in the dark."[4]

Whether we are reading a book, a magazine article, or a research paper, how do we know that what we are reading is reliable and true? Chauncey Sanders, a military expert and historian, wrote in his book *Introduction to Research in English Literary History* that there are three tests for the reliability of a literary

---

4   Norman Geisler, *Christian Apologetics* (Ada, Michigan: Baker Academic Publishing, 2013).

document: (1) Internal Evidence – what the document claims for itself, (2) External Evidence – how the document aligns itself with facts, dates, and persons, and (3) Bibliographical Evidence – the textual tradition from the original document to the copies and manuscripts we possess today.[5]

Internally, the Bible was written over a span of sixteen hundred years, or forty generations. It was written by more than forty men from different walks of life. For example, Moses was educated in Egypt and became a prophet among the Israelites, Joshua was a military general, Daniel was a prime minister, Peter was a simple fisherman, Solomon was a king, Luke was a doctor, Amos was a shepherd, Matthew was a tax collector, and Paul was a rabbi as well as a maker of tents. All the writers had vastly different occupations and backgrounds.

The Bible was written in many different places; it was actually written on three different continents: Asia, Africa, and Europe. Moses wrote in the desert of Sinai, Paul wrote in a prison in Rome, Daniel wrote in exile in Babylon, and Ezra wrote in the ruined city of Jerusalem. It was written under many different circumstances. David wrote during a time of war, Jeremiah wrote at a sorrowful time of Israel's downfall, Peter wrote while Israel was under Roman domination, and Joshua wrote while invading the land of Canaan.

---

5   Chauncey Sanders, *Introduction to Research in English Literary History* (New York: The Macmillan Company, 1952).

The writers had different purposes for writing. Isaiah wrote to warn Israel of God's coming judgment of their sin, Matthew wrote to prove to the Jewish people that Jesus was the Messiah, Zechariah wrote to encourage a disheartened Israel that had returned from the Babylonian exile, and Paul wrote to address problems in different Asian and European fellowships. In addition, the Bible was written in three different languages: Hebrew, Aramaic, and Greek.

Putting all these factors together, we see that the Bible was written over sixteen hundred years by forty different authors in different places and different languages, under various circumstances, and addressing a multitude of issues. It is amazing that with such diversity, there is such unity in the Bible. That unity is organized around one theme: God's redemption of man and all creation. Hundreds of controversial subjects are addressed, yet the writers do not contradict each

> It is amazing that with such diversity of authors, there is such unity in the Bible.

other at all. The Bible is one incredible document. I can only imagine what you would have if you took just ten authors from one walk of life, from one generation, in one place, at one time, with one mood, on one continent, and with one language – all writing on just one controversial subject. You would certainly have a conglomeration of ideas – anything but harmony. Internally, the Bible has no discrepancies and is in total agreement.

Next, let's move on to the Bible's external evidence – or how the Bible aligns itself with facts, dates, and people. In 1964, the Italian Archaeological Mission, led by Paolo Mathiae, began an archaeological dig at Tel Mardikh in Northern Syria. In 1968, a statue of Ibbit-Lim, king of Ebla, was discovered. From 1974 to 1976, two thousand complete tablets ranging in size from one inch to over a foot, as well as four thousand fragments and more than ten thousand chips, were discovered that were dated to around 2300 BC. In use in Ebla was the name "Canaan," a name critics once said was not used at that time and was used incorrectly in the early chapters of the Bible. Not only this, but names such as Adam, Eber, and Yithro were found, as well as the names of the gods of Ebla, including Dagon, Baal, and Ashtar.

Confounding earlier skeptics, but confirming the Bible, an important discovery was made in Egypt in 1896 by British archaeologist Flinders Petrie at Thebes. A tablet known as the Merneptah Stele, an upright stone slab bearing an inscription serving as a monument, was found that mentions Israel. By the way, Merneptah was a pharaoh who ruled Egypt from 1212-1202 BC. The context of the stele indicates that Israel was a significant entity in the late thirteenth century BC. This is quite significant as it is the earliest extrabiblical reference to the nation of Israel that has been discovered.

The Hittites were once thought to be a biblical legend, although the Old Testament mentions them more than fifty times. This was true until their capital and records were discovered in northern Turkey. The initial discovery by French scholar Charles Texier found the first Hittite ruins in 1834. Then archaeologists such as Hugo Winckler followed up with discovery after discovery. In 1906, Winckler found a royal archive with ten thousand tablets inscribed in cuneiform Akkadian.

The walls of Jericho were discovered in the 1930s by British archaeologist John Garstang. The story of the walls of Jericho falling down is recorded in Joshua 6:1-27. The people of Israel had just crossed over the Jordan River into the land of Canaan (Joshua 3:14-17). This was the land of milk and honey that God had promised to Abraham more than five hundred years earlier (Deuteronomy 6:3; 32:49). After spending forty difficult years wandering in the desert of Sinai, the people of Israel were now on the eastern banks of the Jordan. Their challenge was to conquer the land of Canaan, the Promised Land. However, their first obstacle was the city of Jericho (Joshua 6:1), an unconquerable walled city. Excavations there reveal that its fortifications featured a stone wall eleven feet high and fourteen feet wide. At its top was a smooth stone slope, angling upward at thirty-five degrees for thirty-five feet, where it joined massive stone walls that towered even higher. It was virtually impregnable – but the walls came down when Joshua and his army marched around the walls for seven days straight, and on the seventh day, surrounded the wall, blew their trumpets, and shouted. The archeological dig matches the description of the walls in Joshua 6.

In 1990, Harvard researchers unearthed a silver-plated bronze calf figurine reminiscent of the huge golden calf mentioned in the book of Exodus.

In 1993, archaeologists uncovered a ninth-century BC inscription at Tel Dan. The words carved into a chunk of basalt refer to the house of David and the king of Israel. It was once claimed that there was no Assyrian king named Sargon as recorded in Isaiah 20:1 because this name was not known in any other record. Then Sargon's palace was discovered in Iraq, and his capture of Ashdod, the very event mentioned in Isaiah chapter 20, was discovered recorded on the palace walls. Even more fragments of the stele memorializing the victory were found at Ashdod.

The ruins of Sodom and Gomorrah have been discovered southeast of the Dead Sea. Evidence at the site seems consistent with the biblical account: *Then the LORD rained down burning sulfur on Sodom and Gomorrah* (Genesis 19:24 NLT). The destruction debris was about three feet thick, and buildings were burned from fires that started on rooftops. Frederick Clapp, an American geologist, theorizes that the pressure from the earthquake could have spewed out sulfur-laden bitumen, which is very similar to asphalt and is known to be in the area through the fault line upon which the city rests.[6]

Nelson Glueck, a renowned American rabbi, archaeologist, and president of Hebrew Union College, discovered 1,500 ancient sites. He is quoted as saying, "No archaeological discovery has ever contradicted a biblical reference."[7] Dr. William Albright, an archaeologist, biblical scholar, and philologist, said, "There can be no doubt that archaeology has confirmed the substantial historicity of the Old Testament."[8]

Last, but not least, there is bibliographical evidence. A codex is a set of manuscript pages held together by stitching. It is the earliest form of a book, replacing the scrolls and wax tablets of earlier times. The Masoretic text is not a specific codex, but is rather an umbrella term for what we consider to be the authoritative Jewish/rabbinic text for the Old Testament. In the sixth century, a group of scholars called the Masoretes began to painstakingly keep track of what was to be the proper text of the Bible. They kept rigorous notes in the margins and compared all the existing manuscripts. Due to their outstanding scholarship, it quickly became the absolute authoritative text of the Bible. The Masoretes included everything from the text itself to proper vocalization,

6   Frederick G. Clapp, *American Journal of Archaeology* (Chicago: University of Chicago Press, 1936), 323-344.

7   Nelson Glueck, *Rivers in the Desert* (New York: Farrar, Straus, and Cudahy, 1959), 136.

8   William F. Albright, *Archaeology and the Religions of Israel* (Baltimore: John Hopkins University Press, 1956), 176.

accents, and complete verses with defective spellings. The Masoretes were very meticulous and professionally trained at copying documents. They regarded the very words of God with utmost reverence. For instance, if they were to copy the book of Isaiah, the entire text would be in all capital letters with no punctuation or paragraphs. Upon finishing the copy, they would count the letters and find the middle letter of the book. If it did not match exactly, they would discard it and start a new copy. All the present copies of the Hebrew text are in remarkable agreement.

In the tenth century, as the era of the Masoretes drew to a close, they compiled all of their research throughout the centuries into one single manuscript of the Bible. In the year AD 920, a scribe named Shlomo Ben Buya wrote a manuscript in the true Masoretic tradition in the city of Tiberius, Israel. The manuscript is known as the Aleppo Codex.

In 1947, the Dead Sea Scrolls were discovered in the area of Qumran in Israel. Various scrolls date from the fifth century BC to the first century AD. Historians believe that Jewish scribes maintained the site to preserve God's Word and protect the writings during the destruction of Jerusalem in AD 70. The Dead Sea Scrolls include nearly every book of the Old Testament, and comparisons with more recent manuscripts show them to be virtually identical. The main deviations are the spellings of some individual's names and other insignificant differences.

For example, the Dead Sea Scrolls include a complete book of Isaiah. When rabbinic scholars compared Isaiah 53 of the Dead Sea Scrolls to Isaiah 53 of the Masoretic Text, they found only seventeen letters that differed out of the 166 words in the chapter. Ten of those letters are minor spelling differences (e.g., "honor" and "honour"), four are stylistic differences (such as the presence of a conjunction), and the other three letters represent a different spelling of the word "light." In other words, the differences are completely negligible. Therefore, we conclude that there are no legitimate discrepancies in the text we read today, which is amazing!

> We conclude that there are no legitimate discrepancies in the text we read today.

R. Laird Harris, a church leader, Old Testament scholar, and founder of Covenant Theological Seminary, wrote a book entitled *Can I Trust My Bible?* He wrote, "We can now be sure that copyists worked with great care and accuracy on the Old Testament, even back to 225 BC.... Indeed it would be rash skepticism that would now deny that we have our Old Testament in a form very close to that used by Ezra when he taught the word of the Lord to those who had returned from the Babylonian captivity."[9]

The composition of the New Testament was officially settled at the Council of Carthage in AD 397. However, the majority of the New Testament was accepted as

---

9   R. Laird Harris, *Can I Trust My Bible?* (Chicago: Moody Press, 1963), 67-89.

authoritative much earlier. The first collection of the New Testament was proposed by a man named Marcion in AD 140. Marcion was a Docetist. Docetism is a belief system that says that all spirit is good and all material matter is bad. Therefore, Marcion excluded any book that spoke of Jesus being both divine and human. He also edited Paul's letters to match his own philosophy.

The next proposed collection of New Testament books on record was the Muratorian Canon, dated AD 170. It included all four gospels, thirteen of Paul's letters, 1, 2, and 3 John, Jude, and Revelation, and was ratified by the Council of Carthage in AD 397. An actual manuscript was discovered in the Ambrosian Library in Milan, Italy, by Italian historian Antonio Ludovico Muratori, and was published by him in 1740.

However, history shows that the actual New Testament that we have in modern Bibles was recognized much earlier, and it is an exact reflection of what the manuscripts contained. For example, around AD 95, Clement of Rome quoted from eleven New Testament books. Around AD 107, Ignatius quoted from nearly every New Testament book. Around AD 110, Polycarp, a disciple of John, quoted from seventeen New Testament books. Using quotes from these men, the entire New Testament can be pieced together, with the exception of about twenty-five verses, most of them from John 3. This evidence witnesses to the fact that the New Testament was recognized far earlier than the

Council of Carthage and that the New Testament we have today is the same as what was written two thousand years ago. There is no literary rival in the ancient world to the number of manuscript copies and the early dating of the New Testament. We have 5,300 Greek manuscripts of the New Testament and ten thousand Latin manuscripts. In addition to those, there are nine thousand miscellaneous copies of the New Testament in existence today that were written in Syrian, Coptic, Armenian, Gothic, and Ethiopic – some of which date back almost to Jerome's original translation in AD 384. We also have more than thirteen thousand copies of portions of the New Testament that have survived to our time, and more and more continue to be unearthed.

The Codex Vaticanus is the oldest extant manuscript of the Greek Bible. The Codex is named after its place of conservation, the Vatican Library, where it has been kept since at least the fifteenth century. It is written on 759 leaves of vellum (prepared animal skin, typically calfskin), in uncial letters (a style of calligraphy called Scriptio Continua – written without regular gaps between words), and has been dated paleographically (paleography is the study of ancient forms of writing for dating purposes) to the fourth century, from AD 300-325.

We also have the Codex Sinaiticus, an Alexandrian text-type manuscript written in uncial letters on parchment, dated to the fourth century, from AD 330-360. It is located in London's British Library. These two codices, Vaticanus and Sinaiticus, are two exceptional parchment copies of the entire New Testament from the fourth century.

Earlier still, we have fragments and papyrus copies of portions of the New Testament that date from AD 180-225. The outstanding examples are the Chester Beatty Papyrus and the Bodmer Papyrus II, XIV, XV. From these manuscripts alone, we can construct all of the books of Luke, John, Romans, 1 and 2 Corinthians, Galatians, Ephesians, Philippians, Colossians, 1 and 2 Thessalonians, Hebrews, and portions of Matthew, Mark, Acts, and the book of Revelation.

The Rylands Papyrus, known as Rylands Papyrus P52, is the oldest fragment we have to date. It was found in Egypt and has been paleographically dated to AD 130. This find forced critics to place the fourth Gospel back into the first century, abandoning their earlier assertion that it could not have been written by the apostle John. The Rylands Papyrus is on display at John Rylands University Library in Manchester, England. It contained the following verses from John 18:

Pilate said to them, "You take him and judge him according to your own law." The Judeans replied, "We don't have the legal power to put anyone to death." This was so that what Jesus had said, about how he was going to die, might be fulfilled. So Pilate went back into the headquarters, called Jesus, and said to him, "Are you the king of the Jews?" Jesus answered, "Are you asking this on your own, or have other people told you about me?" Pilate replied, "Am I a Jew? Your own nation and high priests have handed you over to me; what have you done?" Jesus answered, "My kingship does not derive its authority from this world's order of things. If it did, my men would have fought to keep me from being arrested by the Judeans. But my kingship does not come from here." "So then," Pilate said to him, "You are a king, after all." Jesus answered, "You say I am a king. The reason I have been born, the reason I have come into the world, is to bear witness to the truth. Everyone who belongs to the truth listens to me." Pilate asked him, "What is truth?"

These verses happen to be some of the most important verses concerning the truth about God, the Messiah, man, sin, and salvation.

Author And Work	John's Gospel	Herodotus Histories
Author's Lifespan	10-100	C 485-425 BC
Date of Events	27-30	546-478 BC
Date of Writing	90-100	425-420 BC
Earliest Manuscript	130	900
Lapse Event to Writing	<70 yrs.	50-125 yrs.
Lapse Event to Manuscript	<100 yrs.	1400-1450 yrs.

Herodotus's *Histories* is considered the founding work of history in Western literature.

Sir Frederic G. Kenyon, a paleographer (expert in ancient handwriting), wrote a book entitled *The Bible and Archaeology*, in which he wrote, "The interval then between the dates of original composition and the earliest extant evidence becomes so small as to be in fact negligible, and the last foundation for any doubt that the Scriptures have come down to us substantially as they were written has now been removed. Both the *authenticity* and the *general integrity* of the books of the New Testament may be regarded as finally established."[10]

Brooke Foss Wescott, a British bishop and biblical scholar, and Fenton John Anthony Hort, an Irish-born theologian, took twenty-eight years to create their New Testament in the original Greek. They stated: "If comparative trivialities, such as changes of order, the insertion or omission of the article with proper names, and the like, are set aside, the words in our opinion still subject to doubt can hardly amount to more than a thousandth part of the New Testament."[11]

In other words, the small changes and variations in manuscripts do not change any major doctrine; they do not affect Christianity in the least. The message is the same with or without the variation. We have the Word of God!

The universe had a beginning. In contrast, many ancient myths describe the universe as being organized

<hr>

10   Sir Frederic G. Kenyon, *The Bible and Archaeology* (London: George G. Harrap & Co, 1940), 288-289.

11   Brooke Foss Wescott and Fenton John Anthony Hort, *The New Testament in the Original Greek* (New York: Harper & Brothers, 1881) 561.

from existing chaos rather than as being created. For example, the Babylonians believed that the gods who gave birth to the universe came from two oceans. Other legends say that the universe came forth from a giant egg. The antagonists to the faith, as well as the general non-believing community, would have us believe that there are no scientists who believe in God. They say that in the eyes of science, a belief in God is unnecessary.

The Da Vinci Code is a novel by author Dan Brown that explores an alternative religious history. It sold eighty million copies and has been translated into forty-four languages. *The Da Vinci Code* has its storyline "expert" say the following: "The Bible did not arrive by fax from heaven. . . .

> The small changes and variations in manuscripts do not affect Christianity in the least.

The Bible is the product of man, my dear. Not of God. The Bible did not fall magically from the clouds. Man created it as a historical record of tumultuous times, and it has evolved through countless translations, additions, and revisions. History has never had a definitive version of the book."[12] Thankfully, the comment is in a work of fiction – where it belongs.

Secular scientists often look down their noses at those who believe in God, miracles, creation, etc., and they use supposed scientific facts to dispute our belief in the reality of God. However, not all scientists reject the idea

12   Dan Brown, *The Da Vinci Code* (New York: Doubleday, 2003), 231.

of God. There have always been those in the scientific community whose faith in God remained the foundation of their lives, even as they carried out scientific research and discovery. A few of the many examples are below.

Francis Bacon (1561-1626). Bacon is usually considered the man primarily associated with the so-called "scientific method." The scientific method stresses observation and verification rather than philosophical conjecture (the formation of an opinion or a theory without sufficient evidence for proof). Bacon believed that God gave us two books to study: the Bible and nature.

Johann Kepler (1571-1630). Johann Kepler is considered by many to be the founder of physical astronomy. He discovered the laws of planetary motion and established the discipline of celestial mechanics. Some of his contributions to science include conclusively demonstrating the heliocentricity of the solar system (having the sun as the center), devising a method of mapping star movement, and contributing to the development of calculus. Kepler was a Christian who studied in seminary, but following God's leading, ended up teaching astronomy. Kepler coined the phrase and the idea that research and discovery were "thinking God's thoughts after Him," a motto adopted by many later Christian scientists.

Blaise Pascal (1623-1662). One of the greatest philosophers, Pascal is considered the father of the science of hydrostatics – the study of the pressure that fluids exert on other objects. Pascal had much to do with the development of calculus and the theory of probability, as well as the invention of the barometer. However, he was a deeply religious man who thought and wrote much about his faith. He may be best known for what Christians call "Pascal's Wager," which basically asks why anyone would risk living as if there were no God.

Isaac Newton (1642-1727). Who has not heard of Sir Isaac Newton? He is credited with discovering the law of universal gravitation and the three laws of universal motion, and refining calculus into a comprehensive branch of mathematics. Newton was a Christian from his youth, and in later years he wrote extensively against atheism and in defense of the Christian faith. Newton believed that the Bible authenticated itself better than any other historical record ever written.

Samuel F. B. Morse (1791-1872). Morse is probably most clearly remembered for inventing the telegraph. However, he also invented the first camera in America and made the first photographic portrait. Morse was a man deeply devoted to God. The first message he sent over his newly invented telegraph in 1844 was "What hath God wrought!" (a quote from Numbers 23:23). His life was dedicated to loving and serving God. Morse wrote these words shortly before he died: "The nearer I approach the end of my pilgrimage, the clearer is the evidence of the divine origin of the Bible, the grandeur and sublimity of God's remedy for fallen man are more appreciated, and the future is illumined with hope and joy."[13]

Louis Pasteur (1822-1895). Pasteur was a giant in the discipline of medicine and was instrumental in developing the germ theory of disease, among many other significant contributions in the fields of chemistry and physics. His research helped develop vaccines against many diseases. Pasteur helped demolish the evolutionary theory of spontaneous generation of life. Pasteur also discovered, as others experience now, that when one stands up for a belief in biblical creation, secular naturalistic scientists go on the attack.

William Thompson, Lord Kelvin (1824-1907). Kelvin established the scale of absolute temperatures. Such temperatures are given today as "degrees Kelvin." Lord Kelvin also established thermodynamics as a formal scientific discipline and formulated its first and second laws in precise terminology. Kelvin believed that science affirmed the reality of creation. He was a

---

13   Ray Comfort, *Scientific Facts in the Bible* (Newberry, Florida: Bridge-Logos Publishers, 2001), 50.

devout and humble Christian, even as he aggressively engaged in controversy over the age of the earth, denying Darwinism and upholding creation.

Wernher von Braun (1912-1977). Von Braun was instrumental in the development of the German V-2 rocket before migrating to America. He directed U.S. guided missile development for several years before becoming the director of NASA. On the subject of space flight, he once wrote, "An outlook through this peephole at the vast mysteries of the universe should only confirm our belief in the certainty of its Creator."[14]

Francis Collins (1950-present). Director of the Human Genome Project, he has publicly affirmed his belief in God. Collins has expressed the spiritual wonder of scientific research in these words: "When something new is revealed about the human genome, I experience a feeling of awe at the realization that humanity now knows something only God knew before."[15]

I have shared with you some basic internal, external, and bibliographical evidence in order to prove that we can absolutely trust our Bible for its authenticity. The Hebrew and Greek manuscripts, although copies, have been providentially preserved, and the translations that are available are free from theological bias. Therefore,

14   Wernher von Braun, "My Faith," *American Weekly*, February 10, 1963.
15   Mark O'Keefe, "Some on Shuttle Crew Saw God's Face in Universe," *Washington Post*, February 8, 2003.

we can have confidence that the Bible that we read today contains the Scriptures as they were originally written, and they can be read without fear of it having been tainted to support a particular church or doctrine.

The Bible has been inspired by God and contains the books that serve as our authority.

> We can have confidence that the Bible that we read today contains the Scriptures as they were originally written.

The Bible declares that people either die in their sins (John 8:24) or they die in the Lord (Revelation 14:13). How a person dies or the timing of one's death is not what matters most. What matters most is this: will you die in your sins or will you die in the Lord?

WHAT DOES IT MEAN TO DIE IN YOUR SINS?

I am the light of the world; whoever follows me will never walk in darkness but will have the light which gives life (John 8:12). Jesus said, *I am the light of the world.* You have God to thank for everything good in your life and everything good in the world. Without Him, there is no light, no love, no hope, no peace, and no joy. Take Him away, and everything is darkness. Then Jesus said, *Whoever follows me will never walk in darkness.* Imagine that we are all in a dark tunnel. Jesus has a light, and He is coming toward us, walking through the tunnel. If we walk with Him, we walk in His light. But if we refuse to follow Him and walk the other way, His light will get farther and farther away from us, and eventually we will be left in darkness.

That is true in this life, and of course, it is also true in the world to come. Beyond this world, there is a place where Jesus is. Because He is there, it is a world of light and love and peace and joy. But beyond this world, there is also a place where Jesus is not. Because He is not there, it is a world of darkness and hate and turmoil and misery.

When Jesus said, *I am the light of the world; whoever follows me will never walk in darkness but will have the light which gives life*, it was immediately obvious that His audience was not with Him.

They tried to pick holes in what qualified Him to speak. "You are bearing witness about Yourself," they said; or as people today might say, "Well, that's just Your opinion!" The debate is recorded in John 8:13-20, and it sounds much like it does so often today.

The fact remains that you cannot invite yourself into heaven. Jesus said, *I am going away, and you will look for me, but you will die in your sin – where I am going, you cannot come* (John 8:21).

The religious leaders were sure that they were going to heaven (just as most Americans are today), so they said, "We're going to heaven. If we can't go where He's going, He must be going to the other place; maybe He's going to kill Himself."

So Jesus said, *You are from below, I am from above; you are of this world, I am not of this world* (John 8:23). He is saying, "Earth is your home. You don't belong up there in heaven. Heaven is My home. I don't belong here on earth." There is all the difference in the world between us and Jesus. Heaven does not belong to us.

Suppose someone knocks on the door of your house, and you open the door to find a stranger there. You have never seen him before. Before you can say anything, he pushes the door open, brushes past you, walks straight up the stairs, and starts unpacking his stuff in one of the bedrooms.

You ask him, "What do you think you're doing?"

He says, "This is a nice house, and I've decided to live here."

You stand there completely astonished, and you say, "Excuse me, but this is my house. If you don't leave right now, I will call the police."

If you invite me into your house, I could stay there as your guest, but I have no right to stay at your house if you don't invite me. It is entirely a matter of your invitation. If I stay there at all, it will be at your pleasure. Heaven is Jesus's home, and we have no right to it. We are from below. We don't belong there.

Jesus said, *This is why I said to you that you will die in your sins; for if you do not trust that I AM [who I say I am], you will die in your sins* (John 8:24). To die in your sins means to carry your sins into your death with you. Imagine a person moving from life into death. He doesn't know what's happening to him. He is going forward. He is going out. He has no choice in the matter. He knows he can't go back. He is dying in his sins.

He has this awful feeling that he is guilty. All of a sudden, his whole life flashes in front of him and he sees it for what it is – and it's all wrong. All his life, he has suppressed his conscience, acted against it, and kept it down. Suddenly it asserts itself, and he feels sick to his stomach as he feels condemned. Even worse is the fact that he is condemned in the sight of God and is under the curse of God against sin. He sees all of this now. He had not seen it before, but it is clear to him now.

As David Martyn Lloyd-Jones said:

The commandments that he has stifled again and kept down, they begin to speak to him: thou shall not kill; thou shall not steal; thou shall not commit adultery; thou shalt not take the name of the Lord thy God in vain; thou shalt love the Lord thy God and Him only shalt thou serve – and he hasn't done it! And there he is dying, and it all comes back. He is dying in his sins, surrounded by them, in the atmosphere of them. That's his position. And there he glimpses into the future, and he sees flashes of hell and torments and misery. He is filled with a sense of remorse and loathing for the things he's done. He hates himself and feels he has been a fool. He has lived his life without thinking of this – this

most vital thing! He is going out through
the present and into an unknown future.
And he doesn't know, he doesn't understand. Nothing helps him for which he has
lived, and there he sees
these awful things ahead
of him. And I believe
at that point also he is
given a glimpse of heaven and of glory,
but realizes that he's unfit for it. It's clean,
it's pure, it's light, it's holy, and he knows
he wouldn't be happy there. He's never
thought on those things. He has lived for
the opposite. And there is God in His glory
and all this purity and all this worship.
He's not interested. He never has been, and
yet he sees it's wonderful and glorious, but
he's unfit. He can't go there.[16]

> There is nothing
> more tragic than to
> die in your sins.

There is nothing more tragic than to die in your sins.

There are three places in Scripture where the
phrase *die in your sin* or similar is found: Ezekiel 3:20,
John 8:21, and John 8:24.

Ezekiel 3:20 says, *When a righteous person turns
away from his righteousness and commits wickedness,
I will place a stumblingblock before him – he will die;*

---

16   David Martyn Lloyd-Jones, "Two Ways of Dying," https://www.
mljtrust.org/sermons/book-of-john/two-ways-of-dying/.

because you failed to warn him, he will die in his sin;
his righteous acts which he did will not be remembered;
and I will hold you responsible for his death.

Ezekiel was appointed as a watchman by God. He was responsible to speak God's Word and to solemnly warn the people. The prophet was warned that if he did not sound the alarm, if he did not speak to the people and warn them about the coming judgment, then their blood would be on his hands (Ezekiel 33:7-9). The job of the prophet in the Old Testament was a fearful one that involved a tremendous amount of responsibility. It was an office that no one really wanted. It was also a lonely existence. A prophet was the doom-and-gloom guy who usually ended up dying a miserable death, such as the prophet Isaiah, who was sawed in two; or the prophet Zechariah, who was stoned to death; or the prophet Amos, who was bludgeoned with a club – and all by their own people! Why so? The answer is simple: most people do not want the truth. Oh, they might say that they want the truth, but they can't handle it. Reality shows seem so popular today, yet in real life, truth doesn't go over so well.

> *I am going away, and you will look for*
> *me, but you will die in your sin – where*
> *I am going, you cannot come. . . . This is*
> *why I said to you that you will die in your*
> *sins; for if you do not trust that I AM*

[who I say I am], you will die in your sins
(John 8:21, 24).

From these verses, it seems that the phrase *die in your sins* means that the person will, upon physical death, retain all the sin that he has committed, along with the consequences and punishment due for that sin. The result is that the person will undergo eternal punishment. Physical death separates the spirit from the body; spiritual death separates the spirit from God.

Sin is breaking the law of God (1 John 3:4), and sin separates us from God (Isaiah 59:2). So sadly enough, all who do not trust in the sacrifice of Christ will die in their sins. I say "sadly enough" because it doesn't have to be that way. They do not have to have their sins held to their account. Note that it is not saying they will die *of* their sins, but rather *in* them. Their sins will be retained. They

Physical death separates the spirit from the body; spiritual death separates the spirit from God.

will never be freed from them and they will never have eternal life. To me, this is heart-wrenching – especially when it can be avoided.

In John 8:21, the word *sin* is singular, implying from the context that they would die with their guilt of rejecting Jesus. They would be forever prevented from entering heaven, where the Lord was going. It is a solemn truth! Those who refuse to accept Jesus as Savior and Lord will have no hope of heaven. How dreadful to die in one's sins – without God, without Christ, and without hope forever!

In John 8:24, the word *sins* is plural. This implies that the unsaved will die with all of their sins, not just that of rejecting Jesus. It makes sense to say that by the sin of rejecting Jesus, all other sins are retained.

Sin is a legal problem. Since sin is breaking the law of God (1 John 3:4), when we sin, we retain a consequence according to the law. Jesus never broke the law (1 Peter 2:22). Our sin was imputed (legally transferred) to Him on the cross (1 Peter 2:24). Since the wages of sin is death (Romans 6:23) and since Jesus died with those sins, thereby fulfilling the requirement of the law, the legal aspect of the debt of sin is satisfied in the sacrifice of Christ. That is why He could say, *It is accomplished!* (John 19:30). All who receive the sacrifice of Jesus by faith will be justified by that faith (Romans 5:1). Justification is a legal declaration of righteousness before God. Therefore, when people who have trusted in Jesus die, they are not doing so with their sins. They are dying without the legal consequence of their sin. However, all who have not trusted in Jesus by faith will retain the legal consequence of their sin and will suffer the proper punishment according to the law.

You will die in your sin (John 8:21). Singular. One sin. What is that sin? What is the one sin these people are in danger of dying in? *This is why I said to you that you will die in your sins* [plural]; *for if you do not trust that I AM [who I say I am], you will die in your sins* [plural] (John 8:24). *If you do not trust that I AM [who I say I am].* Unbelief toward Jesus Christ is the one sin that causes you to take all your other sins into your death with you. Unless you believe, you will die in your sins. If you turn that around, you have the hope of the gospel. Unbelief toward Christ leaves you to die in your sins, but if you believe that Jesus is the Messiah, you will not die in your sins.

> Unbelief toward Jesus Christ is the one sin that causes you to take all your other sins into your death with you.

Why is believing in Jesus so important? Because faith is the bond of a living union in which you give yourself to Christ and Christ gives Himself to you. Christ becomes your Savior and your friend. Christ becomes your Lord and Master, and when you belong to Him, His home is yours.

There is more. Jesus lived a sinless life. He is the only person who has ever done that or could ever do that. He lived and died without sin. The Bible tells us that *He himself bore our sins in his body on the stake* (1 Peter 2:24). *The Lord laid on him the sins of us all.* (Isaiah 53:6 NLT).

The marvelous thing that is true for every person who has faith in Jesus Christ is that Christ carried your sins into His death so that you won't carry them into yours. Believe in the Lord Jesus Christ, embrace

Him, receive Him, and follow Him (submitting to His will) – and you will not die in your sins. You will die in the Lord! *Blessed are the dead who die united with the Lord* (Revelation 14:13). You may be dying of thirst, but you don't have to die thirsty.

What can be said to a friend or loved one who is not a professed believer and is drawing near to death? I actually had this experience recently. I had a dear friend, a best friend, whom I have known for more than thirty years. We met at a gym where I was work-ing to supplement my ministry salary. Although my friend was a brilliant surgeon and I was just a personal trainer, we developed great respect for one another, as well as a great friendship. Intelligible words will not sufficiently express how I feel about my dearest friend, but if I had to use words to describe him, they would include words such as loving, kind, generous, brilliant, playful, caring, hospitable, funny, and com-passionate. However, we tend to overlook that he was a sinner, and like all of us, he fell short of God's holy requirement to be able to be with Him forever.

After we moved to Georgia twenty years ago to start a congregation, I would visit my friend throughout the year, making frequent trips back to Florida to spend a week at a time with him. I looked so forward to seeing him. He had been gifted with good health, and that's why his cancer diagnosis was a shocker. It came out of left field. One day he was experiencing abnormal levels of pain. The tests showed that he had multiple tumors throughout his body. It is not that I think the gospel has anything to do with Frank Sinatra, but his line from his song "That's life" really applies here: "You're flying high in April, shot down in May." I immediately went to visit him as I had a strong premonition that his sickness would be unto death.

Although he was very gifted, the fact remained that he was a sinner, like all of us, and he desperately needed a Savior. I had literally witnessed to him for thirty years. On the last day that I was in the hospital with him, I just wept at his bedside, for although I prayed ceaselessly, I had a strong intuition that this would be the very last time we would get to talk to each other in this life. He couldn't talk much, but he could listen and understand. Through my tears, I told him that I would be willing to crawl over broken glass on my hands and knees to hear him ask God for forgiveness of his sins and make Jesus his Lord and Savior. I told him that this was the only way to heaven and that I needed to know that I would see him again. I begged him not to die in his sins. I am overjoyed to tell you that he did, in fact, receive Jesus as his Lord and Savior. The Bible says that if you confess with your lips and believe in your heart that Jesus is Lord, you will be saved (Romans 10:9).

The fact of the matter is that there are both choice events and no-choice events in life. For instance, your birth is a no choice event. Your death is a no-choice event. Your resurrection from the dead is also a no-choice event. The choice you do have, though, is in regard to your final destination. The Bible tells us that all people will be raised on the last day. Some will be raised to eternal judgment, and others to eternal blessing. There are two – and only two – choices.

Today, it is all about staying young and maintaining one's youth. We are obsessed with looking good. They say that sixty is the new forty. I say that their math is off. Although I exercise and try to eat right, my body – including my eyes – has been around for more than sixty years now. I recently had an eye exam – something that I hadn't had in a very long time. Therefore, I was not surprised when I was told that I needed reading glasses. I was surprised, though, when I was told to choose a frame for the lenses. I looked up, and to my amazement, I saw hundreds of frames to choose from. I don't enjoy making these types of choices. I wish there were just two frames on the wall – one black frame and one white frame. This is why I love the Bible so much. God made it so easy. You have God and Satan. You have righteousness and unrighteousness, or rightness and wrongness. You have the narrow path that leads to life and the wide path that leads to death. You have heaven and hell. You have the simple choice of the white frames or the black frames.

I implore you to think about your final destination and salvation, or the lack thereof. Three thousand years ago, the Bible informed us that our lifespan is seventy or possibly eighty years (Psalm 90:10), and *after this comes judgment* (Hebrews 9:27).

On an eternal scale, seventy to eighty years is a blip. The Bible says that one day is like a thousand years to the Lord, and a thousand years is like one day

Jesus carried the sins of others into His death so that you do not have to carry them into yours.

(2 Peter 3:8). So if we use a simple algebraic equation, our lives are like an hour and a half on an eternal scale.

Here is the deal: if you have never repented for your sins and never received Jesus for the forgiveness of your sins, then I pray that this would be the day of your salvation.

Jesus said, *I am the light of the world; whoever follows me will never walk in darkness but will have the light which gives life* (John 8:12).

There is a world that is very dark because Jesus is not there. There is also a world that is full of love, peace, and joy because Jesus is its light. Jesus died for sinners just like you and me. Ask Him for mercy. Ask Him to forgive you and cleanse you. Jesus carried the sins of others into His death so that you do not have to carry them into yours.

What about you today? Are you following Jesus? Do you believe that He is the Messiah, the Savior of the world?

Suppose two men die of heart attacks: one dies in his sins and the other dies in the Lord. Which one would be you? Two women die in car accidents: one dies in her sins and the other dies in the Lord. Which one would be you? If you were to die tonight, would you die in your sins or would you die in the Lord?

THE THIEF ON THE CROSS

Two men, both criminals, were led out to be executed with Jesus. When they came to a place called the Skull, Jesus was nailed to the cross. The two criminals were also crucified – one on His right and one on His left. Jesus said, *Father, forgive them; they don't understand what they are doing* (Luke 23:34). The soldiers gambled for his clothes by throwing dice.

The crowd watched and the leaders scoffed. *"He saved others,"* they said, *"so if he really is the Messiah, the one chosen by God, let him save himself!"* (Luke 23:35). The soldiers mocked Him, too, by offering Him a drink of sour wine. They called out to Him, *If you are the king of the Jews, save yourself!* (Luke 23:37). A sign was fastened above Him with these words: *This is the king of the Jews* (Luke 23:38).

One of the criminals hanging beside him scoffed, *Aren't you the Messiah? Save yourself and us!* (Luke 23:39).

But the other criminal protested, *Don't you fear God even when you have been sentenced to die? We deserve to die for our crimes, but this man hasn't done anything wrong.* Then he added, *Jesus, remember me when you come into your Kingdom.* (Luke 23:40-42 NLT).

Jesus replied, "I assure you, today you will be with me in paradise" (Luke 23:43 NLT).

The cross is a place where love and justice met – where all humanity has been weighed and found wanting. There Jesus hung with outstretched arms, suffering for a prodigal world's return. On either side hung two thieves, teetering between life and death, between heaven and hell – until one of them said, *Jesus, remember me when you come as King.*

The crazy thing is that these were the very last words that Jesus heard before He died. They were not words from a religious leader or from one of His disciples, but from a common criminal. The words have a connotation of saying, "Don't forget me," and by implication, they mean, "Please take me where You are going." With the words, *I assure you, today you will be with me in paradise,* that common criminal was lifted off his cross and into the loving arms of the Savior.

We don't know much about the thief. We do know from Matthew's account that he mocked Jesus along with the crowd:

The leading priests, the teachers of religious law, and the elders also mocked Jesus. "He saved others," they scoffed, "but he can't save himself! So he is the King of Israel, is he? Let him come down from the cross right now, and we will believe in him! He trusted God, so let God rescue him now if he wants him! For he said, 'I am the Son of God.'" Even the revolutionaries who were crucified with him ridiculed him in the same way. (Matthew 27:41-44 NLT)

Here is the sixty-four-thousand-dollar question: What was it that caused the one thief to stand up for Jesus and have the humility to submit to Him? He saw something he had never seen before and had never even heard of before. When they hurled their insults at Jesus, He did not retaliate. When He suffered, Jesus made no threats. Instead, He entrusted Himself to God, who judges justly. In the midst of the most excruciating pain known to man, and while suffering for the crimes of others, He appealed to the highest court in heaven and said, *Father, forgive them; they don't understand what they are doing* (Luke 23:34).

The thief was blown away. He turned his head toward Jesus, and I imagine they locked eyes. He felt as if Jesus could see all the way to the very depths of his soul. He felt as if Jesus knew him better than he knew himself, and everything was exposed. In that moment, time stood still. In Jesus's eyes, the thief saw no hatred, no contempt, and no judgment. He saw only one thing: forgiveness. At that moment, the thief realized that Jesus was no ordinary man.

The thief did not know much about theology. However, he did know that Jesus was a king, that His kingdom was not of this world, and that this king had the power to bring even the most unworthy people into His kingdom. In an intimate moment with the Savior, a lifetime of moral debt was canceled.

It is amazing to think about. Amid the humiliating mockery of the crowd and the horrific pain of the crucifixion, Jesus was still about His mission to seek and save the lost (Luke 19:10). The good news is that Jesus is still about His mission even now. Like the thief, we all have stolen much. When we have raised our voice in anger, we have stolen from another's peace. When we have immoral thoughts, we have stolen from

> We all stand before the Lord exposed in our thievery. We are all guilty.

another's dignity. When we have hurt someone's feelings, we have stolen from their self-worth. When we have spoken the truth without love, we may have stolen from the kingdom by pushing a soul further away from the borders of paradise.

We all stand before the Lord exposed in our thievery. We are all guilty. If you have not yet done so, confess it all to the only one who can take it all. Why die in your sins? Let Him wipe your spiritual slate clean, and be filled with power from on high – power that can not only change your heart, but can also change the world. Ask the Lord Jesus to remember you, and you, too, will be with Him in paradise.

YOU DON'T HAVE TO
DIE IN YOUR SINS

God is fully good, fully loving, fully beautiful, and fully true – and these characteristics continually flow out of Him. The love, grace, goodness, and beauty of the Lord were so full that they flowed out of Him in the creation of a good and beautiful world. God brought this beautiful world into existence, and as the crowning glory of His good work, He created people in His image so that they could share in His love, grace, and goodness.

When God created people, He also gave them free will, for love allows the object of that love to make choices. Only robots, computers, and machines don't have choice. God gave us the choice to either receive and live in His love or to reject it. Giving people free will dignified their choices and recognized the image of God within them. After God created the first humans,

Adam and Eve, He told them that everything was available to them, but there was only one thing that they were not to do. They were not to eat from just one specific tree in the garden. Sadly enough, when they were tempted, they fell prey to that temptation, and they crossed the line. Not only did it cause a feeling of separation, remorse, shame, and, worst of all, guilt, but it opened the door to more sin, which would cause our world to go into a downward spiral that has continued ever since.

But this is not the end of the story. Not only is God good and loving, but He is also all-knowing and all-powerful. God didn't react, but He was proactive – with a plan He had in place before He laid the foundations of the world. God did not want people to live in brokenness, darkness, and separation from Himself, so He made a plan that would set the broken world right so that people could be forgiven, healed, restored, and made whole. Jesus the Messiah, fully God, became fully human and showed people God's love in His sacrifice on the cross. Jesus willingly gave His own life as a sacrifice to pay for our sins. After three days, Jesus rose from the dead, not only demonstrating God's ultimate power over sin and death, but also letting us know that if we believe, we, too, will be resurrected when the kingdom comes.

People still physically die, but because Jesus conquered sin and death, followers of Jesus will experience eternal life with Him well after their physical death. Their bodies may die, but they will be resurrected into eternal life with Jesus.

I used to see signs in many different places that said "John 3:16." I saw them at Olympic stadiums, sports arenas, billboards, etc. As a boy raised in Orthodox Judaism, I had no idea what it meant or what it was referring to. Now as a believer, I would say that it is probably the most famous sentence in all of literature. It says, *For God so loved the world that he gave his only and unique Son, so that everyone who trusts in him may have eternal life, instead of being utterly destroyed.*

When you really stop and think about this, it is absolutely mind-boggling, for it is God's kindness that leads us to repentance (Romans 2:4). The verse that follows John 3:16 is not as well-known, but it is just as impor-tant. John 3:17 says, *For God did*

> God has gone to the utmost length and cost in order to save man.

not send the Son into the world to judge the world, but rather so that through him, the world might be saved.

God is not a harsh, cruel ruler eager to pour His anger on mankind. Rather, His heart is filled with tenderness, and He has gone to the utmost length and cost in order to save them. He could have sent His Son into the world to condemn the world, but He did not. On the contrary, He sent Him to suffer, bleed, and die so that the world through Him might be saved. The work of Jesus on the cross was of such tremendous value that all sinners everywhere can be saved if they will receive Him.

I spent a number of years lifeguarding. I don't know of anyone who would not extend their hand to a lifeguard in order to be saved if they were drowning. The key to this is to first realize that you are drowning. Most people are doing well enough in their own eyes that they do not see themselves going underwater. They are so full of themselves that they won't admit that they are going under for the third time, so they refuse to cry out, "Save me!" Don't wait until you are on your deathbed to look for a lifeguard. I am pleading with you today to receive Jesus into your life. He is the only lifeguard you really need. Please confess your sins, believe in your heart that Jesus died for you, and declare with your lips that Jesus is Lord and Savior. Not only will you have eternal life in the world to come, but you will have abundant life in the here and now. Please don't die in your sins!

Let's Make a Deal is a TV game show that first aired in the United States in 1963 and has since been replicated in many nations across the globe. When I was a little boy, we had only three channels on which to watch television programs. Game shows were a lot of fun to watch, and I tended to root for the underdog, as I usually still do.

The structure of *Let's Make a Deal* includes the host interacting with selected audience members, known as "traders." Typically, a trader is given a valuable item and is then faced with the decision to either keep it or swap it for a mystery item. The essence of the game lies in this mystery - the trader does not know if the concealed item is of equal or greater worth, or if it's a "zonk," a prize of minimal or no value to the trader.

At the end of the show, the host chooses three people who are willing to give up their prizes in order to try to trade for the "big deal of the day." Each contestant who agrees chooses one of three doors that are offered. The host asks the first contestant, "Do you want door number one, door number two, or door number three?" The next contestant chooses between the two remaining doors, and the final contestant gets assigned the only remaining door. Unfortunately for one individual, behind one of the doors is always a zonk or a booby prize.

With God, though, we know what is behind the doors, and the choice is much easier because there are only two doors to choose from. If you choose door number one, you get Jesus as your sacrifice for the forgiveness of your sins, and you get the big deal, not just of the day, but for all eternity. If you choose door number two, you do not get Jesus and His sacrifice for the forgiveness of your sins, but you die in your sins for all eternity – the ultimate zonk.

I know it seems too easy, but when you truly come to grips with your wrongdoing and your selfishness, and when you come to grips with the pain and suffering you have caused others, you have feelings of guilt, which is good – for this leads to repentance and change. You come before God and take Him at His word that He will wash you clean and give you a new heart. The miraculous happens when you choose to follow Him. He will change you from the inside out. He will empower you and direct you so that you can go from being a zonk to being His big deal – not so much in terms of your own glory, but in terms of being used by Him to change the spiritual climate of the entire universe.

Don't ask me how He does it. There are things that defy explanation, mysteries that are too deep to fathom, and strange circumstances that puzzle the keenest of intellect. All I know is that I was the king of selfishness, preoccupied with self, and now I live for others and even put other people before myself. A great change has happened in me, and I'm loving it! Please choose door number one – and don't die in your sins!

ABOUT THE AUTHOR

Rabbi Greg Hershberg was born in New York City and raised in Orthodox Judaism. He graduated Pace University, Magna Cum Laude and later owned and operated an executive search firm in New York City, specializing in banking and finance. In 1989, he married Bernadette and while on his honeymoon in Israel had a visitation from the Lord that turned his heart to serving God.

In 1992, Rabbi Greg became involved in the Messianic Jewish Movement and was ordained through the International Association of Messianic Congregations and Synagogues (IAMCS). He became the leader of Beth Judah Messianic Congregation. In 2002, the Lord moved Rabbi Greg and his family to Macon, Georgia, to lead Congregation Beth Yeshua.

The ministry went global in 2010 and Congregation Beth Yeshua became Beth Yeshua International (BYI). What was a local storefront congregation became an international ministry/training center in Macon, Georgia, with congregations and schools in India, Kenya, Ethiopia, Australia, Germany, Israel, and across America. In addition, Rabbi Greg's messages are live-streamed throughout the world.

Rabbi Greg currently resides in Macon, Georgia, with his wife, Bernadette, and their four children. More about Rabbi Greg can be found in his autobiography, *From The Projects To The Palace*.

www.bethyeshuainternational.com

Watch Greg Hershberg's testimony with One for Israel Ministry

Things God Hates, Things God Loves
by Greg Hershberg

Scripture says that the Lord will *look with favor* on the one who is humble and contrite and who trembles at His Word. This word *look* in Hebrew is nabat, and it means "to regard, to consider, or to pay attention to." In plain words, we're told that the God-fearing person who *hates what He hates and loves what He loves* is the one the Lord pays favorable attention to.

To experience the favor of God is amazing and incredible, to say the least. Journey through this book with me and consider the Scriptures that tell us what the Lord hates and what He loves. Ask the Lord to teach you to live with all your heart, soul, mind, and strength for Him, in such a way that He will look upon you with favor.

Available where books are sold.

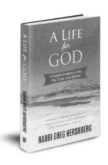

A Life for God, by Greg Hershberg

To grasp the depth and height of the great I AM and to live life with the end (eternity) in sight is a believer's most significant accomplishment. Within each of His chosen people, God has placed a desire to know Him, to worship Him, and to live victoriously for Him. He has shown us how to have the right perspective concerning this life and the one to come. And what God starts, He finishes.

Come, let Messianic Rabbi Greg Hershberg open the Torah and give you glimpses of the incredible love and character of our God. Let him point you to the Savior through the offerings of Leviticus and the mournful lament of Psalm 22. Let him guide you through the greatest commandment as you learn to say "no" to yourself, pick up your execution-stake, and follow the great I AM.

Available where books are sold.